RHYTHMIC HEART

लय हृदय

SURAJ VATSAL

Dedicated to mind

Contents

1. WORDS OF WISDOM

Words of wisdom
It never ever ends
Neither the thoughts
Nor the action it mends
Oh the sense of knowing
Unknowingly it lends
Throughout the expedition
A map never seen
For my own journey
No one has here been
For the revealings, because
Solace it will mean
How can I mistake
Petals for the thorn
Fulfilment of moments
But ages to mourn
And the times it had died
Once more it's reborn…

2. DEEDS

There's something
Which needs to be done
Among those thousands
I don't know even one
And unknowingly the sequence
Seems to have begun
Where's the doer
If I had imagined none
Drops of river
Making the stride
Waves of ocean
Creating the tide
Who the rider
When time's the ride
Lifetime of achievements
But why the mundane pride
Amongst the millions desire
And billions of deeds
When did you decide
That the doing leads
In the happening of happenings
The outcome pleads
While guilt of mind
Perpetually it builds…

3. WHO IS IT?

Who is it
Yeah right here
Barely appreciable
Confused identity
A male or female
Or a veil of ignorance
A product of programming
In pursuit of unending belonging
To continue the myth
To continue to dream
Holding on to what he can
Yet slipping everything again
Trying hard and getting insane
Continuing with so much pain
Oh, its a human mind
Not even a tangible object
Yet takes so much pride
Strong sense of identity
Fatally furious over rejection
Not even a visible thing
But something which thrives on
Continues attempts to prove itself
The existence and grandeur
And yet a complete delusion
Delusion of being the form

Delusion of being the cause

4. PEACE

There I was and all of us
Different in a million ways
Alas so same to mindful gaze
Struggling for existence in similar stage
From dumbest of beauty to ugliest of brain
Waiting for the journey that already began
I was busy delving and so were they
In the stream, daydreaming the dream
Irrespective of which boots in they stand
Oblivious to vision which never expand
Worrying for some reason they brought
Which they understand they thought
Yet some chatting and feeling they know
And some busy in devices that glow
Here comes the train and horn they blow
We ride hastily and here we go
The train is on move but we never do
Because our deeds still continue
Some were listening and some had to say
Yet some busy in a lonely way
With similar phenomenon passes multiple Station
In delusion of nearing destination
Feet's Running in and feet moving out
Thoughts moving in and thoughts fading out
Silently creeps in but occasionally they shout

It's happening here and nobody sees
Missing the trunk in a jungle of trees
Like a mirror which wants to hideout
You just show their petty pride pout
Hence the mind hiding behind
Erupting thoughts bizarre of multiple kind

5. LONGING FOR LOVE

Longing for love,
To be loved
Desired and needed
Feel the importance
To be approved of
The deficient self
Finding reasons to
Be proved Otherwise
Cloaking it as a need
Or as a birthright
Or loneliness as an evil
It looks for the same
Self righteousness
To be proved what it is exactly deficient in
But that's a mere escape
More lies to cover a lie
More stupidity to potray as wise
And the naked truth
Revealing shamelessly

6. DON'T ASK THE NAME

Don't ask the name
We are just the same
Pumping hearts
Racing minds
Burning desires
Disgusting lies
All identical pursuits despite
Different shoe sizes
Foolish failures of Grand goals
Same tears same cries

7. DEATH

Someone dies
Infront of my eyes
Jostling the mind
And all its lies
But hardly ever
anything penetrates
Over and over
its foolishness accumulates
The grand true death
Here it misses again
And the body burns
Turns ash in vain
It has an eternal myth
That it knows it all
Its already deep dug
The pit to desperate fall
The grass is green
And sky is blue
Mind busy dreaming
For it has no clue..

8. ACCEPT ME

Think about me
Fancy in your dreams
Feel the need
And the futility instead
Let my absence hurt you
Lemme grasp your thoughts
Cast a Mojo
In your deeds and dreams
Let me prevail
Like a veil
Over the sun
And let this overshadow
It's own glory
And then I would call it love
And may be it gets rewarded..

9. THE WAIT…

So hapless

Helplessly it waits….

Through the karma tantrums

Weathers of the old and new

Repetitive sequences and processes

Seriousness of miseries

Humours of incompetent death

The futility of importance

Dualities of choices

Impotent happenings and

tiring punctuality of the clocks

Just for a moment of bliss

and beyond…

10. A WHOLE NIGHT

A whole night of dreams
the days full of delusion
And the question remains
When is the conclusion
Has it ever learnt
That it can never know
When it never has had
the chance to outgrow
An ocean of stupidity
And mountain of lies
In between the blooming valley
Of dancing fireflies
Existence limited to alas
Meagre idea of existence
And heaps of eternal dirt
Waiting for the eternal storm..

11. NOTHING OTHERWISE

Nowhere to go

Nothing to do

Nobody to be

Lest the physical compulsions

But the grand facade

The unending perseverance

Of excellence and ambitions

The infinite wrapping of ideas

Over minuscule existence

And nothing otherwise….

12. WHERE IS THE GOD

Where's the God
I want to see
Do you know any better?
Then let it be
When the master is lost
There is no sojourn
Lend me some insight
Or let it patiently earn
In the cacophony of emotions
A deafening silence grows
Amidst the precious revelations
the Ego heart throws
And remains the vacuum
Which can never be filled
Can it ever overcome overnight
The karma it build?

13. THE EMPTY BOWL

A new day begins with the old son sun, alas!
Accustomed 'Holy Grail' of his palm crease,
A beggar on the pavement sits with,
With bright eyes full of hope,
And the luck conspiring over his innocence again,
My empty bowl is never full,
And the hope never dies,
In the search of enigmatic fulfillment,
Like waiting endlessly,
A circle trying to merge in centre,
Give it hope and it endures a day more,
Dreaming of grandiosity in the dark,
And the day for the rude truth,
The pattern goes on and on,
The same carol on every Christmas,
Like the needy very need,
Bowl- the very emptiness- inseparable and non other,
An absolute underdog of divine establishment,
Sees it sooner,
Or looses illusion quite later…

14. अटल

मत रोको बूँदों को बारिश की
माटी में मिल जाने से
आ जाएगा वरना सैलाब
ऐसे ही तरसाने से
तीनों दशाएँ झेल चुका हूँ
ऐ मलमल में सोने वालो
समंदर का तूफ़ान उठा है
जग जानेगा भीगंने वालो
राह है लम्बी हार ना माने
मिटि जाए पर रुक ना जाने
साँसों का क्या आये जाये
जिसके मध्य ब्रह्म को ठाने
ऊपरवाले ने दिया नहीं
हमने भी फ़िक्र किया नहीं
चलते हैं अपने पैरों पर
विश्वास किसी का लिया नहीं

15. अमृत

अमृत को देके

कर दो किनार

बंजर में भटका

तेरे ही द्वार

लीला की लप्सिा में

लपिटा संसार

राहत की चाहत में

ठोकर हज़ार

नभि जाता अब सिर्फ़

रस्मो ंसे प्यार

रिहाई की नही ंनौबत

उम्र कैद में जीते कारागार

निद्रा हैं भूख हैं

साँसो ंका सुख हैं

विचारो ंकी दैनन्दिनी

पड़ी हैं बेकार

आकर के प्रकार में

तू निहित निराकार

कर दू समर्पति

मेरे ंमन का विकार

16. अवज्ञा

जीते रहे ज़िन्दगी
और बढ़ाते रहे उमर
आँखों में आ गई मोतिया
अपितु सत्य ना आया नज़र
इधर का उधर करते रहे
और किया बस उधर का इधर
सांस स्वर्ण को व्यय करके
अहंकार ही संचय किया मगर
पोखर पी के बुझ गई प्यास
खलियान खा के भर लिया पेट
मृत्यु नाम की चारपाई
पर आके अब जा लेटे
बुझा के दीपक ज्ञान का मानुष
मिटा के मन का चिर कौतुहल
करते रहे अवज्ञा हठ तुम
जीवन लक्ष्य विमुख अविरल

17. उपकार

कभी प्रेम बन के भीगा दिया
कभी जुनून बन के नभा दिया
ग़लतियों की हर सज़ा को
अश्रु कारागार में क्षमा दिया
दुर्भावना उपेक्षा की परीक्षा
चरि तंद्रा से पृथक की इच्छा
अभिमान के आसमान में
शशि-निश्छल सूरज खिला दिया
प्रार्थना दी, समर्पण, हठ
ज्ञान, योग, भक्ति की कृपा
और ब्रह्म ने अनायास ही
भ्रम-पाषाण को डिगा दिया।

18. कविता

पंक्तियों की पंक्ति से
लो हो गया निर्माण
कविता का जन्म हुआ
और साहित्य का सम्मान
गद्य के स्वर हैं ये
या शब्दों के वाण
विच्छेद किये अनभिज्ञता के
बनि कोई निपुण कृपाण
भगवद् की हैं गीता
और गीता का हैं ज्ञान
द्विज ने उसको पढ़ लिया जो
गढ़ लिया अभिमान
भाव की हो शून्यता
दक्चक्षु करे प्रत्यक्ष
चित्त को आये ना समझ
आए लेखनी समक्ष

19. जंगल का फूल

जंगल का फूल
खिलि के मुरझाया
कसिी से ना पूछा
ना कसिी को बताया
भटकती रही जन्दिगी
फूलो के जैसी महक
जसिने कयिा पैदा
उसी का नहीं हक.
साँसें रहीं आते
तो आती रहें जायें
मेरा क्या है मतलब
मुझे ही ना बतायें
नदी की है नयिति
समुद्र की ओर
रेत से ना पूछो
कि जाना कसि छोर....

20. द्वविधा

प्रधानता का पाखंड
और वविषता प्रचंड
वद्विता का बोध
नर्बिद्धधिका घमंड
वज्ञिान का संशय
वश्विास का दंभ
नयिति की द्वविधा
कर्त्तव्य का लौह स्तंभ
लेखनी की तत्परता
कन्ति्प्रबोध का वलिम्ब....

21. फ़क़ीर

दुनिया का मेला है
मेले में भीड़
संकट में फँस गया
वैरागी फ़क़ीर
गठरी भी खाली है
गजोदर की भाँति है
मैली चादर में लिपटा
ये अदना शरीर
रोशनी भी पूछे अब
तू है कितना अमीर
रोटी की क़ीमत है
छप्पर का दाम
दौलत के बाज़ार ने
किया बदनाम
पीछे पड़ी माया थी
आगे मेरे राम
मन को ना चैन है
तन को ना मिला आराम
दोषी ये मनवा है
ढूँढे है ज्ञान
जिसके कुछ नसीब नहीं
उसका क्या सम्मान
क़िस्मत एक पत्थर है

मलिता उधार
चमके तो हीरा है
वरना माथे बोझा बेकार
काहे का शोर है
जब तक ये भोर है
काली मेरे रात की
उपहार अंधकार

22. संशय

उपरोक्त का तात्पर्य
और नम्रिन का अभिप्राय
वर्णों की पंक्तियों के
अनुच्छेद का पर्याय
शब्दों की प्रचुरता
भावों की अभाव
चिंतन के आलेख में
कपटता का प्रभाव
स्वर के संगीत में
सुरों की पराधीनता
ताल के उद्वेग में
वाद्य की वनिम्रता
यथार्थ की दुर्लभता में
संभावनाओं की दुर्बलता
जीवन अर्थ उद्देश्य प्रबल पर
चरित्र की संकीर्णता

23. ससिकयाँ

साँस ले ली जी लिया
आँख नम थी पी लिया
रंग लाल रक्त की
जम गई थी धमनियाँ
ख़्वाहिशों की तितलियाँ
झड़ चुकी पंखुड़ियाँ
मर गई उम्मीद की
फूल सब की कलियाँ
साँसों के बोझ तले
दबी दबी सी ससिकयाँ
दर्द के थकान की
मिट चुकीं स्मृतियाँ
मृत्यु हाथ थाम कर
चल मुझप उपकार कर
न फिर शुरू जो हो सके
ऐसा तू अंजाम कर..

www.ingramcontent.com/pod-product-compliance
Lightning Source LLC
Chambersburg PA
CBHW021157130726
47988CB00004B/1647